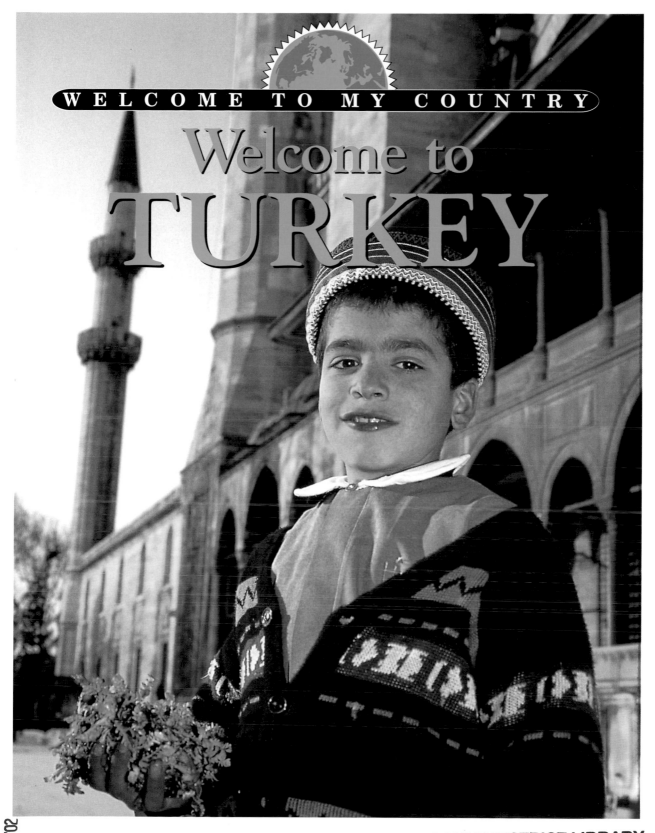

WELCOME TO MY COUNTRY

Welcome to
TURKEY

Gareth Stevens Publishing
A WORLD ALMANAC EDUCATION GROUP COMPANY

Written by
VIMALA ALEXANDER/NERIMAN KEMAL AND SELINA KUO

Edited in USA by
DOROTHY L. GIBBS

Designed by
GEOSLYN LIM

Picture research by
SUSAN JANE MANUEL

First published in North America in 2002 by
Gareth Stevens Publishing
A World Almanac Education Group Company
330 West Olive Street, Suite 100
Milwaukee, Wisconsin 53212 USA

Please visit our web site at:
www.garethstevens.com
For a free color catalog describing
Gareth Stevens Publishing's list of high-quality
books and multimedia programs,
call 1-800-542-2595 or
fax your request to (414) 332-3567.

© **TIMES MEDIA PRIVATE LIMITED 2002**
Originated and designed by
Times Editions
An imprint of Times Media Private Limited
A member of the Times Publishing Group
Times Centre, 1 New Industrial Road
Singapore 536196
http://www.timesone.com.sg/te

Library of Congress Cataloging-in-Publication Data
Alexander, Vimala.
Welcome to Turkey / Vimala Alexander, Neriman Kemal,
and Selina Kuo.
p. cm. — (Welcome to my country)
Summary: An overview of the geography, history, government,
economy, people, and culture of Turkey.
Includes bibliographical references and index.
ISBN 0-8368-2541-1 (lib. bdg.)
1. Turkey — Description and travel. [1. Turkey.] I. Kemal, Neriman.
II. Kuo, Selina. III. Title. IV. Series.
DR429.4.A44   2002
956.1—dc21   2002017720

Printed in Malaysia

1 2 3 4 5 6 7 8 9 06 05 04 03 02

PICTURE CREDITS
Agence de Presse ANA: 22
Archive Photos: 13, 15 (bottom), 36,
    37 (both)
Art Directors and Trip Photo Library: 1, 7,
    14, 18, 19, 20 (bottom), 24, 25, 29, 32,
    33 (bottom), 38, 40 (both), 41
Camera Press Ltd.: 15 (center)
Haga Library, Japan: 30, 33 (top)
The Hutchison Library: 17
Images of Africa Photobank: 26
International Photobank: 2, 3 (bottom),
    4, 6, 27, 31, 45
John R. Jones: 9, 10, 23
Nazina Kowall: 3 (center), 8, 11, 21, 35, 39
North Wind Picture Archives: 12, 15 (top)
Christine Osborne Pictures: 28
Topham Picturepoint: 16
Nik Wheeler: cover, 3 (top), 5, 20 (top), 34

Digital Scanning by Superskill Graphics Pte Ltd

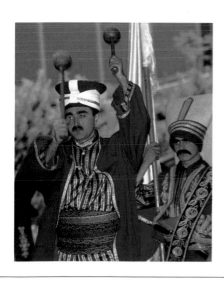

Contents

Words that appear in the glossary are printed in **boldface** type the first time they occur in the text.

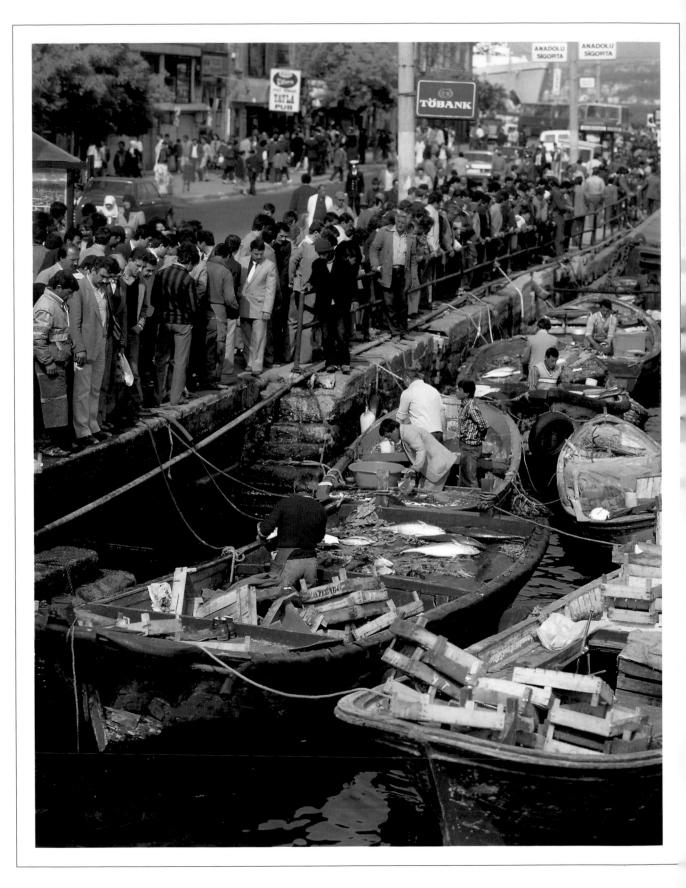

Welcome to Turkey!

Modern Turkey was founded in 1923. The country has a long and rich history formed by the many **civilizations** that **flourished** there, including Persians, Greeks, and Romans. Lying between Europe and Asia, Turkey has a **unique** blend of Eastern and Western cultures. Let's explore Turkey and its **heritage**.

Opposite: A crowd of Turks is waiting on a **quay** in Istanbul to buy fresh fish.

Below: Kabob shops are a common sight in Istanbul and many other Turkish cities.

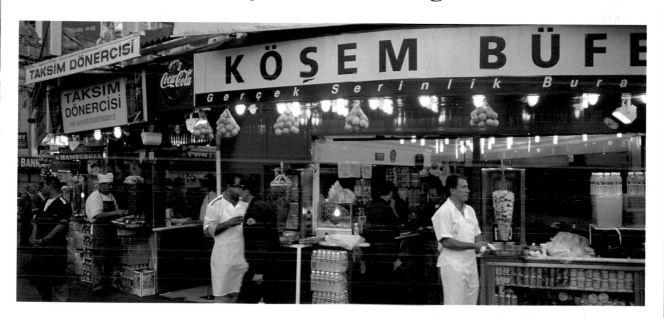

The Flag of Turkey

The current Turkish flag was adopted in 1936. It has a red background with a white **crescent** and a white five-pointed star. The crescent and the star are Muslim symbols. Several legends suggest reasons why they appear on the flag.

The Land

Turkey is shaped like a rectangle, with an area of about 301,400 square miles (780,626 square kilometers). To the east, it is surrounded by the countries of Georgia, Armenia, Azerbaijan, Iran, Iraq, and Syria. Greece and Bulgaria lie along its northwestern border. The country has coastlines on three seas, and mountain ranges run **parallel** to both its northern and southern coasts.

Below: Turkey's beautiful western coastline is on the Aegean Sea. The country also has coastlines on the Mediterranean Sea to the south and on the Black Sea to the north.

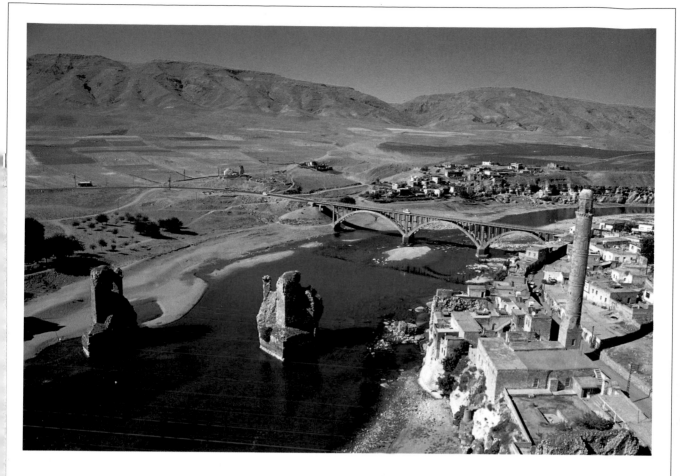

Western Turkey's coastal plains are important farming areas. Central Turkey is a high **plateau**, called the Anatolian Plateau. It reaches from the northern Pontic mountain range to the southern Taurus range. Eastern Turkey has as many as eleven more mountain ranges, and they include the country's highest peak, Mount Ararat, at 16,950 feet (5,166 meters). Turkey's largest lake, Lake Van, is also in the east.

Above: The Tigris River flows through several of Turkey's eastern provinces. The Euphrates is another major river in eastern Turkey.

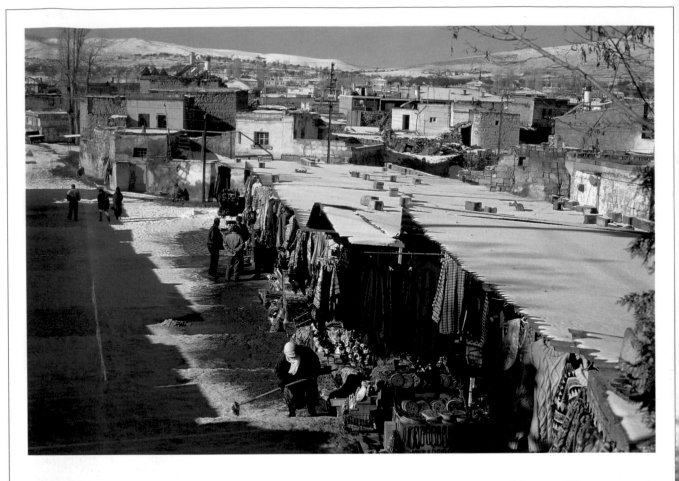

Climate

Different parts of Turkey have different climates. While the coastal areas have mild winters and summers, the central plateau has more extreme temperatures. The average temperatures in the city of Istanbul, on the coast of the Sea of Marmara, range from 43° Fahrenheit (6° Celsius) in winter to 75° F (24° C) in summer. In centrally located Ankara, Turkey's capital, temperatures range

Above: The souvenir shops in Turkey stay open even in very cold weather.

from 26° F (–3° C) in winter to 86° F (30° C) in summer. With bitterly cold winters and hot, dry summers, eastern Turkey has the most extreme climate.

Plants and Animals

Grasslands cover much of central and eastern Turkey and the area northwest of the Sea of Marmara. Thick forests grow in most of the rest of the country. Wild animals in the forests include bears, deer, leopards, and boars. Water buffalo and camels are farm animals.

Below:
Some hillsides in northeastern Turkey are bare because the logging industry has cut down so many trees.

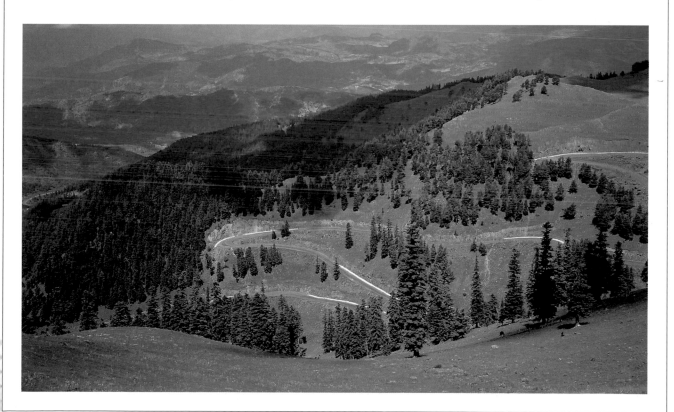

History

Ancient Turkey was called Anatolia. Signs of human life in parts of Anatolia date back to 9000 B.C., but the Hittites were the first major civilization. They settled in Anatolia in about 1900 B.C. Not much is known about the Hittites except that they came from the northeast and ruled until about 1200 B.C. After the Hittites, a series of different kingdoms ruled Anatolia until 546 B.C.

Below: Copies of ancient drawings show us what life might have been like in Hattusas, the Hittite capital.

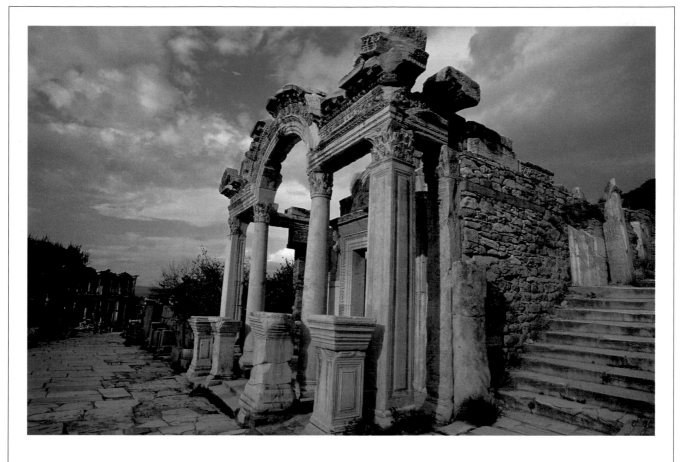

Anatolia was part of the Persian Empire from 546 B.C. to 334 B.C., when it fell to the Greeks. In 133 B.C., it came under Roman rule and thrived as part of the Byzantine Empire. The Seljuks, who were Turkish warriors, invaded Anatolia in A.D. 1071 and took control of its central and eastern regions. The Byzantine Empire did not end, however, until Constantinople (now Istanbul) fell to the Ottoman Turks in 1453.

Above: These ruins in the province of Izmir were once an ancient palace.

The Ottoman Empire

The Ottoman Turks first established themselves in Anatolia in the 1330s. By 1453, they had full control of the country. Their empire grew to include parts of Europe, the Middle East, and Africa, but religious and economic problems during the 1500s weakened it. The empire struggled for centuries, trying to recover, until World War I (1914–1918) caused its final downfall.

Above: Mustafa Kemal (1881–1938) introduced many **reforms** in Turkey. In 1934, the Turkish parliament gave him the name "Atatürk," or "Father of Turks."

The Turkish Republic

After World War I, the **Allies** began to divide the Ottoman Empire among themselves. When the Ottoman ruler did not try to stop them, angry Turks started a **nationalist** movement led by a military hero named Mustafa Kemal. The nationalists drove out both the Allies and the Ottoman government. The Republic of Turkey was founded on October 29, 1923, with Ankara as its capital and Kemal as its president.

Opposite: This drawing illustrates the day the Ottoman Turks took control of Constantinople.

World War II and After

In World War II (1939–1945), Turkey sided with the Western **democracies**. Its own government was a democracy until the Turkish army took control in 1960. For the next twenty years, the Turkish government alternated between military and **civilian** rule. In 1983, the country returned to civilian rule and has been a democracy ever since.

Above: The Atatürk monument in the city of Istanbul was built in honor of Mustafa Kemal, Turkey's national hero.

Süleyman the Magnificent (1494–1566)

In 1520, Süleyman I was crowned King of the Ottoman Empire. During his reign, he encouraged the growth of art and literature and introduced a system of laws. His great deeds earned him the nicknames "the Magnificent" and "the Lawgiver."

Süleyman I

Tansu Çiller (1946–)

Turkey's first female prime minister, Tansu Çiller, improved the country's economy. She was appointed in 1993, but she resigned in 1996 because of conflicts within her government.

Tansu Çiller

Ahmet Necdet Sezer (1941–)

Turkey's top judge, Ahmet Necdet Sezer, became the country's tenth president in May 2000. Sezer is the fourth civilian to serve as president. He firmly supports democracy and human rights.

Ahmet Necdet Sezer

Government and the Economy

The Turkish parliament, or Turkish Grand National Assembly (TGNA), has 550 members who are elected by Turkish citizens. Each member serves a five-year term. The members of the TGNA elect Turkey's president, who serves a seven-year term. The president appoints the prime minister, who is usually the leader of the party with the most TGNA representatives. The prime minister selects a Council of Ministers that must be approved by the president.

Left: The Turkish parliament house is located in the city of Ankara, Turkey's capital.

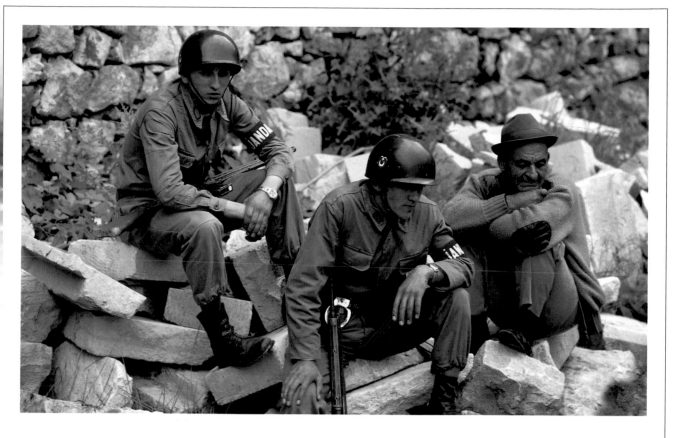

The Council of Ministers appoints a governor to supervise each of Turkey's eighty provinces. Each governor must be approved by the president. People in rural areas elect a village chief and a council of elders to govern them.

Above: All Turkish men between the ages of twenty and forty-nine must go through at least eighteen months of military training.

Between 1960 and 1980, Turkish armed forces, which include Land Forces, the Navy, the Air Force, the Coast Guard, and armed police, took over the government three times to safeguard democracy in the country.

The Economy

Almost half of the people in Turkey's workforce have jobs in farming. The country's main **cash crops** include cotton and grains such as wheat, rice, corn, and barley. Farmers in Turkey also grow many fruits and vegetables, including olives, cabbage, and grapes.

Rich natural resources, especially boron, copper, and chromium ore, are important to Turkey's economy, too.

Above: These women remove husks from corn to earn a living.

Textiles, petroleum, and iron are important export industries in Turkey, but services, such as banking, tourism, and telecommunications, bring in over half of the country's annual earnings.

Visitors to Turkey are attracted by the intriguing cultural mixture of East and West, as well as the historical sites, beautiful landscapes, and rare religious architecture. Large Turkish cities, such as Ankara and Istanbul, are particularly popular tourist destinations.

Below: Every year, millions of tourists visit Turkey's many archaeological and historical sites.

People and Lifestyle

About 80 percent of Turkey's more than 66 million people have Turkish **ancestors** who came to Anatolia from central Asia. Another 15 percent of the population are Kurds, Turkey's largest **minority group**. Their ancestors were **native** Anatolians. Smaller minority groups in Turkey include Armenians, Greeks, and Arabs, and Istanbul has a large Jewish community.

Above:
Kurds look the same as Turks and belong to the same religion, but they have their own language and traditions.

Left: The ancestors of some Turks were from **nomadic** tribes, such as the Seljuks.

Traditional Values

Although Atatürk's reforms introduced a modern and freer lifestyle in Turkey, many people, especially in the eastern provinces, have kept their traditional values and customs and still live by strict religious rules.

Turkish law gives men and women equal rights. Men, however, typically hold a more important position than women in society, especially within families. Even today, few women in Turkey work outside the home.

Above: Most Turkish women still honor their Islamic faith by covering their heads when they are out in public.

Family Life

In the past, three generations of Turks lived together as a family — a married couple, their unmarried daughters, their sons, their sons' wives, their unmarried granddaughters, their grandsons, and their grandsons' wives. When a woman married, she became a member of her husband's family. Today, most Turkish families include only a married couple and their unmarried children, but every member works in some way to help support the family.

Above: Today, large, traditional families are more common in eastern Turkey than in other parts of the country.

A Turkish wedding used to be very elaborate, with a religious ceremony and a feast that involved months of preparation. Since Turkey became a republic, these kinds of weddings are held only in rural areas.

The birth of a baby has always been a time for celebrating in Turkey. A new mother receives gold jewelry, and the baby is showered with expensive gifts.

Left:
Modern weddings in Turkish cities are usually simple civil ceremonies.

Education

From preschool through high school, education is free in Turkey. Children between the ages of four and six may attend preschool, but it is not required. Most Turkish children start school at the age of seven. They must complete five years of elementary school and three years of middle school. In rural areas, where middle schools are scarce, many children are required to attend only elementary school.

Below:
Turkey has about 46,000 elementary schools for children between the ages of seven and eleven.

After middle school, students may choose to attend either high school or vocational school. High schools, called *lycées* (lee-SAYS), offer a three-year course of study to prepare for college. Vocational schools offer four years of job-related training in fields such as business, agriculture, and nursing. University education is limited. Only students with very high scores on a national entrance exam are accepted.

Above:
The University of Istanbul is one of Turkey's four major universities.

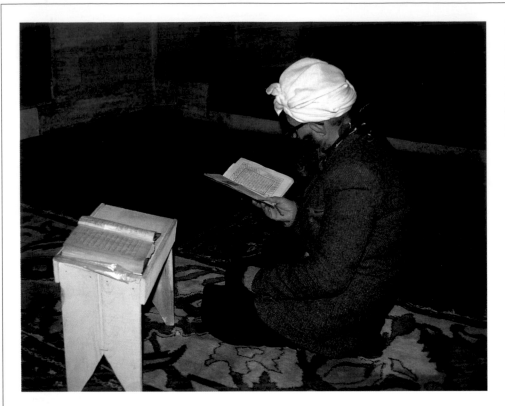

Religion

Islam is Turkey's main religion. More than 99 percent of the population are Muslims. Following the five pillars of Islam, Muslims worship one God, called Allah. They pray to Allah five times a day, give **alms**, and **fast** during the holy month of *Ramazan*, known as *Ramadan* in other Islamic countries. Every Muslim is also expected to make the *hajj* (HAHGE), a holy **pilgrimage** to Mecca, at least once.

The law in Turkey allows religious freedom but forbids involving religion in politics. Public preaching is against the law, yet the government pays for the upkeep of mosques and provides religious education in public schools. Although many Turkish Muslims do not strictly follow Islamic law, most keep the Islamic holy day on Friday and celebrate the religious holidays Seker Bayram and Kurban Bayram.

Below: The Blue Mosque in Istanbul is named after the special blue tiles that were used to build its interior.

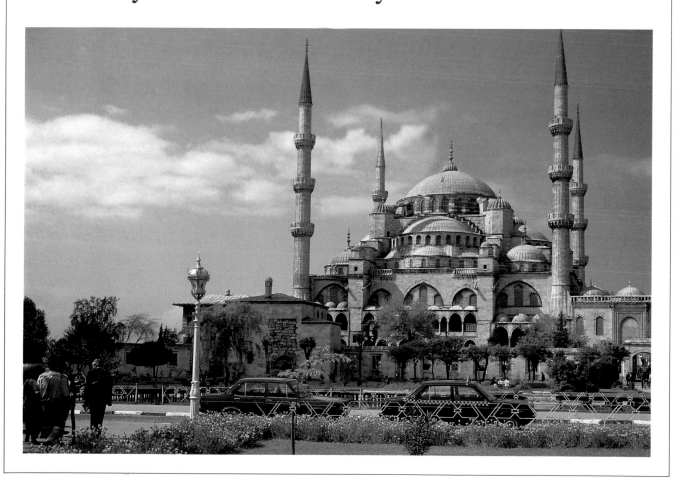

Language

Turkey's main language is Turkish. Other languages include Armenian, Arabic, Kurdish, and Greek, but over 90 percent of the population speaks Turkish. The Seljuks introduced this language back in the eleventh century. During Ottoman rule, Arabic elements were added, and the language became known as Ottoman Turkish. Early in the 1900s, Atatürk replaced the Arabic alphabet with the Roman alphabet.

Left: *Milliyet* is one of Istanbul's two major newspapers.

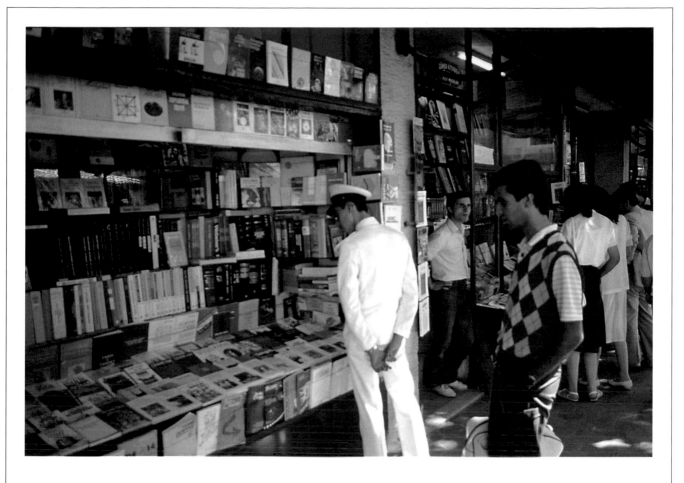

Literature

Much of Turkey's early literature was about religion, while modern Turkish authors write about the country and its problems. Famous Turkish authors include Yasar Kemal (1923–) and Orhan Pamuk (1952–). Kemal's 1955 book *Ince Memed* is published today in more than thirty countries. Pamuk's award-winning books are published in thirteen different languages.

Above:
Bookstores are popular in Turkey, where storytelling has long been part of the culture.

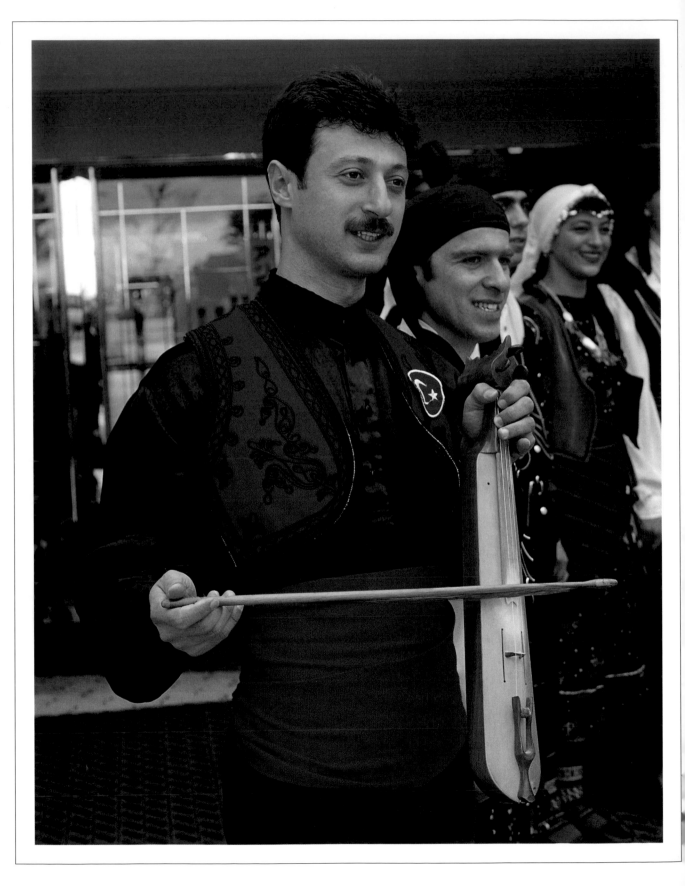

Arts

Music

Turkish music reflects the country's history and ranges from traditional classical and military forms to lively belly-dancing music. The classical music of Turkey uses notes that create a "flat" sound. The military music is very loud. Ottoman bands used drums, clarinets, and cymbals to drown out the sounds of battle. Belly dancing is performed at weddings and parties, as well as in many restaurants.

Opposite: The *kemençe* (kuh-MAHN-chay) is a traditional Turkish instrument. It looks like a fiddle and is played with a bow.

Crafts

An amazing variety of handicrafts can be found in Turkey's famous **bazaars**. The small shops at these bazaars sell handmade lace, embroidered fabrics, baskets, pottery, and even donkey's milk! "Evil eye" charms are especially popular items. Made of blue-and-white glass or ceramic, they are believed to protect their owners from harm.

Below: Colorful handmade slippers are among the craft items for sale at Turkey's bazaars.

Shadow-Puppet Theater

Shadow-puppet plays are an important art form of Turkey's folk culture. The plays' two main characters are named Karagöz and Hacivat. One popular legend claims that they were created in memory of two fourteenth-century laborers. An angry Turkish ruler killed the laborers when their mischievous pranks kept his building from being completed on time. Shadow-puppet performances use jokes and humor to make statements about social issues.

Left:
During a shadow-puppet performance, a light is placed in front of the small, colorful puppets to cast large shadows onto the curtains behind them.

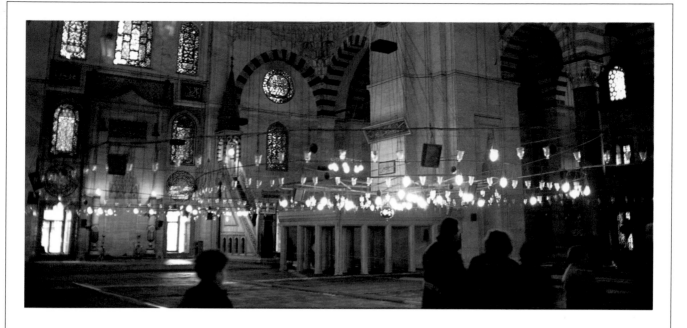

Architecture

Most Turkish architecture is based on the simple but elegant designs of buildings constructed during the Ottoman Empire. Mimar Koca Sinan (1489–1588) was the greatest Ottoman architect. Sinan designed more than 260 buildings and influenced almost every Turkish architect after him. The Mosque of Süleyman in Istanbul is one of his most famous designs. It is the largest mosque built by the Ottomans and has schools, a hospital, stables, shops, and even a cemetery inside it.

Above: The Mosque of Süleyman is a stunning example of Mimar Koca Sinan's architectural talent.

Above: Detailed Ottoman tilework decorates the inside of Topkapi Palace, which was built in the mid-1400s.

Leisure

Whether dancing, enjoying a meal, or just visiting, Turks like to spend time with their families and friends. They especially like getting together with people at coffeehouses. Turkey has coffeehouses everywhere. They

were even there in Ottoman times, when coffee was nicknamed "the milk of chess players and thinkers." Today, Turks still meet over a cup of coffee or tea to talk about world events, play backgammon, or exchange stories.

Above:
Good storytellers can always find an audience in Turkish coffeehouses.

Turkish Coffee and Tea

Although Turkish coffee, or *kahve* (KAH-vay), is famous all over the world, Turks actually prefer to drink tea, or *cay* (CHYE). They drink it in small, tulip-shaped glasses, without sugar or milk. The tea is kept hot all day without ever letting it boil, so

it never becomes bitter. The taste of kahve ranges from fairly bitter to very sweet. Sugar is added while the coffee is brewing to achieve the desired level of sweetness. Turkish coffee is thick and is served in tiny cups.

Above: Coffee was probably brought to Turkey in about 1555, so coffeehouses have long been a part of Turkish life.

Sports

Soccer is Turkey's most popular sport. The country has hundreds of teams, with games being played every week. Turkey's national teams also play in international competitions. Galatasaray Spor Kulübü, the most famous Turkish team, won the 1999/2000 Union des Associations Européennes de Football (UEFA) Cup against Britain's Arsenal.

Below: Enthusiastic Turkish soccer fans fill the stadiums for almost every match in the country's larger cities.

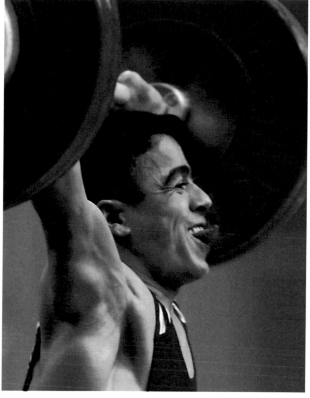

Wrestling, Turkey's second most popular sport, has a long history in the country. In fact, some of today's wrestling techniques, such as the turk, the sarma, the eyerk, and the künde, were developed by Turkish wrestlers of the past. Yasar Erkan won Turkey's first Olympic gold medal in wrestling at the 1936 games in Berlin. Turkey now has about 4,000 wrestlers. Adali Halil, Celal Atik, and Salih Bora are famous world champions.

Above:
Soccer midfielder Ahmet Yildirim (*left*) tries to score a goal for the Galatasaray team in the finals of the 2000 Turkish Cup competition. Halil Mutlu (*right*) won a gold medal in weightlifting at the 2000 Olympics in Sydney, Australia.

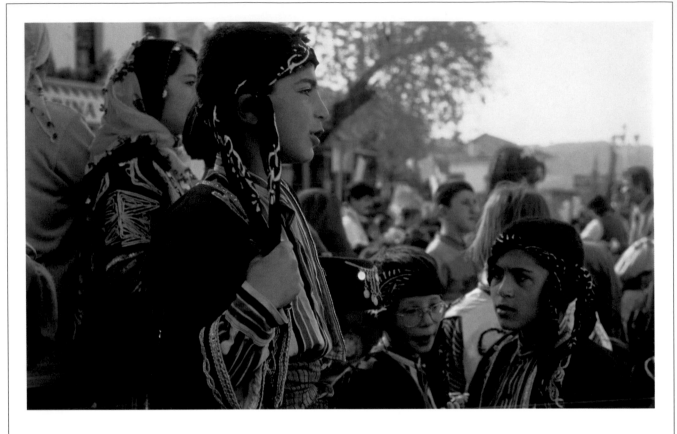

National Holidays

April 23 is a special day in Turkey. It is National Sovereignty Day, a major national holiday honoring the day in 1920 when the country's government changed from an Islamic state to a parliamentary democracy. April 23 is also Children's Day, recognizing the importance of children to the nation's future. Two other national holidays in Turkey are Victory Day on August 30 and Republic Day on October 29.

Above:
Some children put on traditional Turkish clothing to celebrate National Sovereignty Day and Children's Day, which are both on April 23.

Festivals

Every year, in April, May, and June, the Istanbul Foundation for Culture and Arts hosts three separate festivals to promote local and international artists in film, theater, and music.

Each January, Turkey has a camel wrestling festival in Selçuk. In this unusual event, colorfully decorated camels wrestle each other until one of them falls down or runs away.

Below: At a camel wrestling festival, the camels' mouths are tied closed so the animals cannot bite each other during the fight.

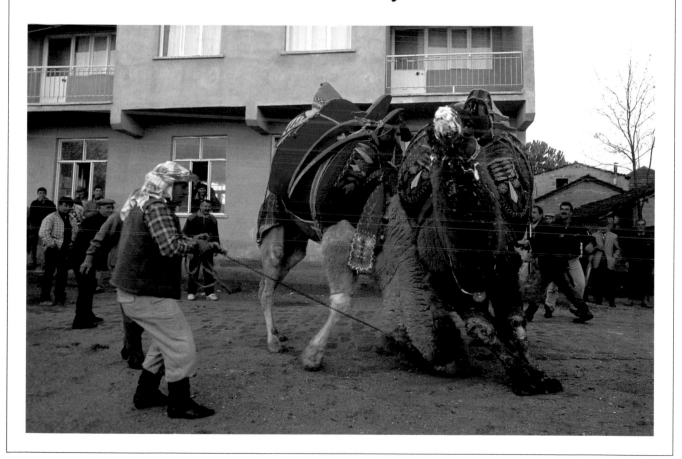

Food

Turkish cooking commonly includes meat, especially lamb. A popular meal called *meze* (meh-ZEH) has a variety of grilled meats and vegetables. They are served with *humus* (HUH-muhs), a chickpea dip, and *haloumi* (hah-loo-MEE), which is grilled goat cheese.

Breakfast is usually fresh bread, spread with jam, honey, or butter or eaten with salty black olives, tomatoes, cucumbers, and cheese. Lunch is the largest meal, while dinner is light.

Above: Many meals in Turkey end with a sweet dessert. Fresh fruits, pastries, and puddings are particularly popular.

Left: The meat for *döner* (DOH-nuh) kabobs is roasted slowly on an upright skewer. Thin slices are shaved off as the meat cooks.

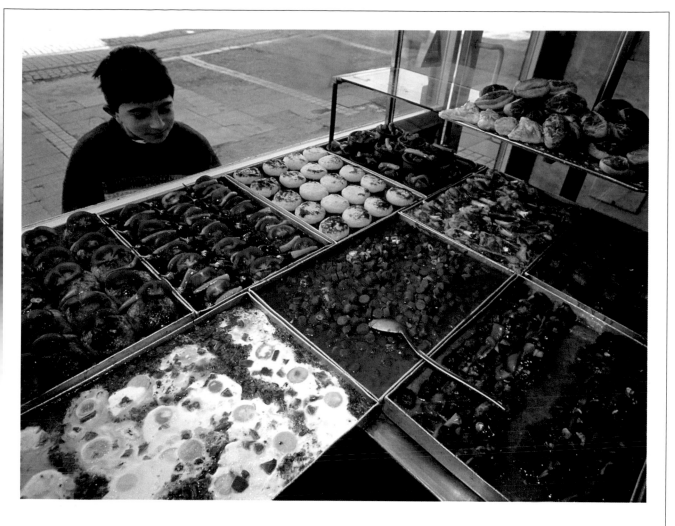

Kepaps (kuh-PAHPS), or kabobs, came from the nomadic Seljuk Turks, who roasted their meat over open fires. Shish kabobs are cubes of meat and vegetables that are grilled on skewers. Döner kabobs are made by roasting thick layers of lamb on a large vertical skewer, then cutting off thin slices to eat with bread and yogurt or humus.

Above: A Turkish deli has a delicious selection of foods. Turkey is one of only a few countries in the world that produces more than enough food for its people.

	A	B	C	D

Aegean Sea A2–A3
Anatolian Plateau B2–D3
Ankara C2
Armenia F1–F2
Azerbaijan F2

Black Sea B1–E2
Bulgaria A1–B1

Catalhüyük C3
Cyprus C4

Ephesus A3
Erzurum E2
Euphrates (river) E2–F4

Georgia E1–F1
Greece A1–A3

Hacilar B3
Hattusas C2

Iran F2–F3
Iraq E4–F4
Istanbul B2

Lake Egridir B3
Lake Van F2–F3

Mediterranean Sea A4–D4
Middle Taurus Mountains C3–D3
Mount Ararat F2
Mount Erciyes D3
Mount Hasan C3

North Anatolian Fault B2–F2

E F

RUSSIA

GEORGIA

ARMENIA

Mount Ararat
(16,950 ft/5,166 m)

●Erzurum

AZERBAIJAN

IRAN

Lake
Van

Tigris

IRAQ

Euphrates

SYRIA

TURKEY

PROVINCES

1	Edirne	**27**	Karabuk	**54**	Kilis
2	Kirklareli	**28**	Ankara	**55**	Giresun
3	Tekirdag	**29**	Konya	**56**	Trabzon
4	Istanbul	**30**	Kastamonu	**57**	Gumushane
5	Yalova	**31**	Çankiri	**58**	Bayburt
6	Çanakkale	**32**	Kirikkale	**59**	Erzincan
7	Balikesir	**33**	Kirsehir	**60**	Tunceli
8	Bursa	**34**	Aksaray	**61**	Elazig
9	Izmir	**35**	Karaman	**62**	Adiyaman
10	Manisa	**36**	Içel	**63**	Sanli Urfa
11	Kutahya	**37**	Sinop	**64**	Rize
12	Usak	**38**	Çorum	**65**	Artvin
13	Aydin	**39**	Yozgat	**66**	Erzurum
14	Denizli	**40**	Nevsehir	**67**	Bingol
15	Mugla	**41**	Nigde	**68**	Mus
16	Kocaeli	**42**	Samsun	**69**	Diyarbakir
17	Sakarya	**43**	Amasya	**70**	Batman
18	Bolu	**44**	Tokat	**71**	Mardin
19	Bilecik	**45**	Kayseri	**72**	Ardahan
20	Eskisehir	**46**	Adana	**73**	Kars
21	Afyon	**47**	Ordu	**74**	Igdir
22	Isparta	**48**	Sivas	**75**	Agri
23	Burdur	**49**	Malatya	**76**	Bitlis
24	Antalya	**50**	Kahraman Maras	**77**	Van
25	Zonguldak	**51**	Osmaniye	**78**	Siirt
26	Bartin	**52**	Gazi Antep	**79**	Sirnak
		53	Hatay	**80**	Hakkari

Pontic Mountains
    C2–E2

Russia E1–F1

Sea of Marmara
    A2–B2
Selçuk A3
Sivas D2
Syria D3–E4

Taurus Mountains
    B3–F3
Tigris (river) E3–F4
Troy A2

Western Taurus
    Mountains B3–C3

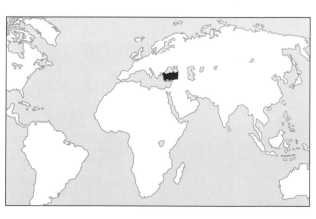

Quick Facts

Official Name   Republic of Turkey

Capital   Ankara

Official Language   Turkish

Population   66,493,970 (July 2001 estimate)

Land Area   301,400 square miles (780,626 square km)

Highest Point   Mount Ararat (16,950 feet/5,166 m)

Important Rivers   Euphrates (776 miles/1,249 km)
                           Tigris (326 miles/525 km)

Largest Lake   Lake Van (1,452 square miles/3,761 square km)

Mountain Ranges   Pontic Mountains (north)
                           Taurus Mountains (south)

Major Religion   Islam

Important Holidays   National Sovereignty Day (April 23)
                           Children's Day (April 23)
                           Victory Day (August 30)
                           Republic Day (October 29)

Currency   Turkish Lira (1,414,000 TL = U.S. $1 as of 2002)

Opposite: Handmade dolls in Turkish costumes are popular souvenirs.

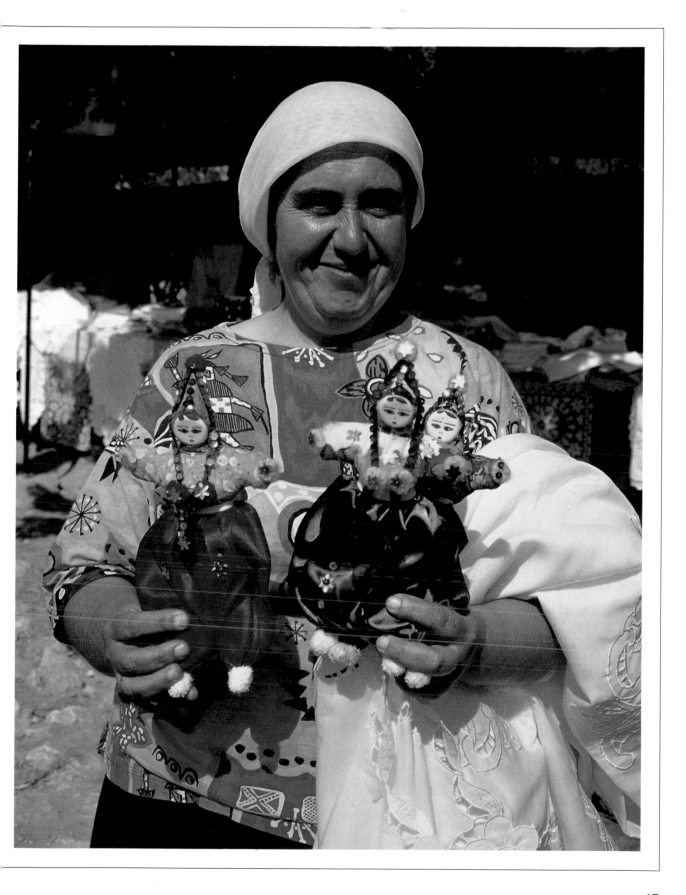

Glossary

Allies: the nations that fought together against Germany and the other Central Powers in World War I.

alms: charitable gifts of clothing, food, money, or other items to help the poor.

ancestors: the members of families who lived in earlier times; past generations.

bazaars: marketplaces that sell local items in small shops or open stalls that are usually lined up along a street.

cash crops: grains, fruits, vegetables, and other agricultural products that are grown in large amounts to be sold.

civilian: relating to people who are not part of a police force or the military.

civilizations: societies that have highly developed cultures and governments and documented histories.

crescent: a thin, curved moon shape.

democracies: governments that are ruled by the people through their elected representatives.

fast: go without any food or some kinds of foods, often for religious reasons.

flourished: grew to be strong and healthy or successful.

heritage: anything that is passed down from ancestors to later generations.

minority group: a small, cultural or social group of people who have the same race, religion, political beliefs, physical features, or other characteristics, which are different from most other people in the larger society to which they belong.

nationalist: devoted and loyal to one nation over any other.

native: belonging to a certain place by being born there.

nomadic: relating to groups of people who have no permanent home and move together from place to place.

parallel: lying in the same direction as something else, but at a certain distance away that is approximately the same at any point.

pilgrimage: a journey to a holy place to show religious devotion.

plateau: a large area of flat land that is high above sea level.

quay: a concrete or stone wharf, or dock, where ships and boats are loaded and unloaded.

reforms: changes that correct faults or make improvements.

unique: one of a kind; different, with nothing else like it.

More Books to Read

Daily Life in Ancient and Modern Istanbul. Cities Through Time series. Robert Bator (Lerner)

Kurds. Endangered Cultures series. Ann Carey Sabbah (Smart Apple Media)

Letters Home from Turkey. Lisa Halvorsen (Blackbirch)

Me and My Shadows: Shadow Puppet Fun for Kids of All Ages. Elizabeth Adams and Dr. Bud Banis (Science & Humanities Press)

Muslim Mosque. Places of Worship series. Angela Wood (Gareth Stevens)

A Treasury of Turkish Folktales for Children. Barbara K. Walker (Linnet Books)

Turkey. Festivals of the World series. Maria O'Shea (Gareth Stevens)

Turkey: Between East and West. Exploring Cultures of the World series. Louise R. Miller (Benchmark Books)

Turkey in Pictures. Visual Geography series. Steve Feinstein (Lerner)

Videos

Splendors of the Ottoman Sultans. (Kulturvideo)

Turkey: The Enchanted Land of Cappadocia. (World Alamanac)

Turkey: West Coast of Turkey, Central Turkey. (Questar)

Turkish Coasts: Istanbul. (Education 2000)

Web Sites

turktour.com/turkey.html

www.smm.org/catal/

www.turkey.org/artculture/

www.turkishodyssey.com

Due to the dynamic nature of the Internet, some web sites stay current longer than others. To find additional web sites, use a reliable search engine with one or more of the following keywords to help you locate information about Turkey. Keywords: *Anatolia, Ankara, Atatürk, Constantinople, Istanbul, Kurds, Ottoman Empire, Turkish.*

Index